INTRODUCTION

Welcome back to FastTrack®!

Hope you enjoyed *Drums 1* and are ready to play some hits. Have you and your friends formed a band? Or do you feel like soloing along with the audio tracks? Either way, make sure you're relaxed…it's time to jam!

The eight songs in this book appear in the order of their difficulty. With the knowledge you already have, you're ready to play them. But it's still important to remember the three Ps: **patience**, **practice**, and **pace yourself**.

As with *Drums 1*, don't try to bite off more than you can chew. If you're tired, take some time off. If you get frustrated, put down your sticks, relax, and just listen to the audio tracks. If you forget something, go back and learn it. If you're doing fine, think about charging admission.

CONTENTS

ABOUT THE AUDIO

Again, you get audio tracks with the book! Each song in the book is included, so you can hear how it sounds and play along when you're ready.

Each audio example is preceded by one measure of "clicks" to indicate the tempo and meter. Pan right to hear the drum part emphasized. Pan left to hear the accompaniment emphasized.

To access audio visit:
www.halleonard.com/mylibrary
Enter Code
6148-7794-1007-8186

ISBN 978-0-7935-7416-2

7777 W. BLUEMOUND RD. P.O. BOX 13819 MILWAUKEE, WI 53213

Visit Hal Leonard Online at
www.halleonard.com

LEARN SOMETHING NEW EACH DAY

We know you're eager to play, but first we need to explain a few things. We'll make it brief...

Melody and Lyrics

All of the melody lines and lyrics of these great songs are included for your musical pleasure (and benefit). These are shown on an extra musical staff, which we added above your part.

Unfortunately, drummers never play the melody (we can't imagine why not?!), but this added vocal line will help you follow the song more easily as you play your part.

And whether you have a singer in the band or decide to carry the tune yourself, this new staff is your key to adding some vocals to your tunes.

Several of the songs have some interesting little symbols that you must understand before playing. Each of these symbols represents a different type of ending.

Endings

1st and 2nd Endings
You know these from Drums 1 (the brackets with numbers):

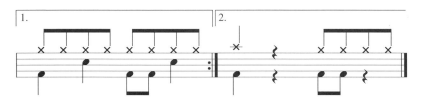

1st and 2nd Endings
When you see these words, go back and repeat from this symbol: 𝄋

Play until you see the words "To Coda" then skip to the Coda, indicated by this symbol: ⊕

Now just finish the song.

That's about it! Enjoy the music...

You Really Got Me

Words and Music by Ray Davies

Wild Thing

Words and Music by Chip Taylor

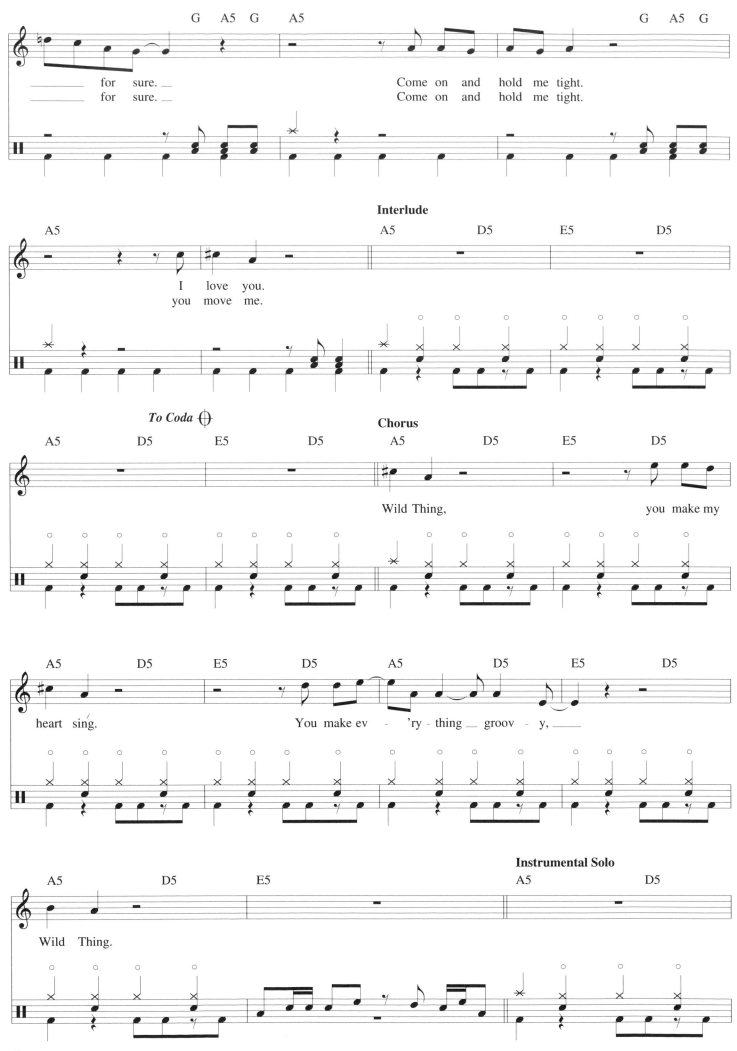

6

I Want to Hold Your Hand

Words and Music by John Lennon and Paul McCartney

Wonderful Tonight

Words and Music by Eric Clapton

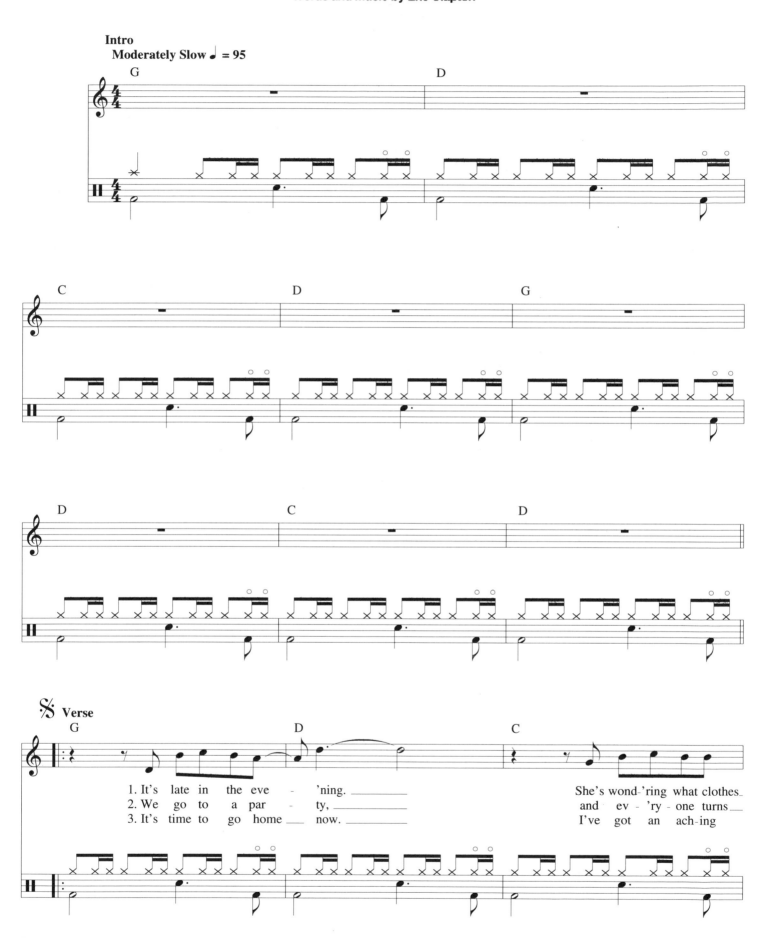

1. It's late in the eve - 'ning. _____ She's wond-'ring what clothes_
2. We go to a par - ty, _____ and ev - 'ry - one turns_
3. It's time to go home ___ now. _____ I've got an ach - ing

She puts on her make - up
this beau-ti - ful la - dy
I give her the car keys,

and brush-es her long blond hair.
is walk-in' a - round with me.
and she helps me to bed.

And then she asks
And then she asks
And then I tell

"Do I look al - right?"
"Do ya feel al - right?"
as I turn out the light,

And I say,
And I say,
I say, "My

To Coda

"Yes, you look won - der - ful to - night."
"Yes, I feel won - der - ful to - night."
darlin', you are won - der - ful to - night."

D.S. al Coda

Oh, my dar-lin', you are

Outro

won-der - ful ____ to-night. ____

Your Song

Words and Music by Elton John and Bernie Taupin

mon-ey, _____ but,   boy, if __ I   did, ____   I'd buy _ a big

house where ___   we both _ could   live.

live.   And you __ can tell

ev - 'ry-bod - y   this _ is your   song. ___   It may _ be

quite ___ sim - ple, but   now that it's done, _____

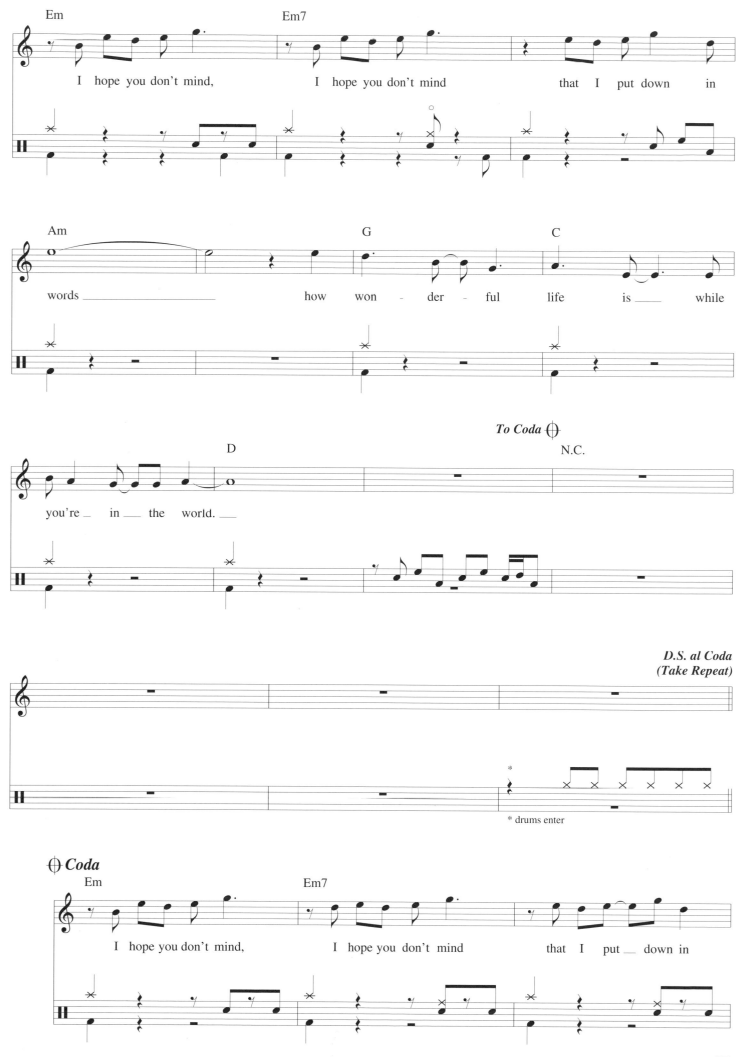

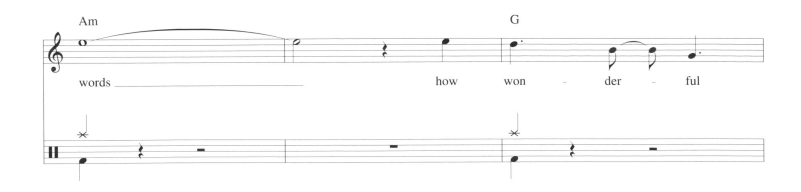

words _____ how won - der - ful

Outro

life is ___ while you're ___ in ___ the world.

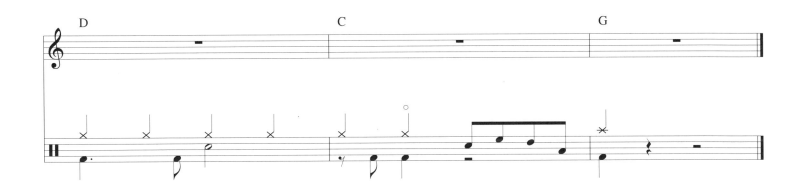

Additional Lyrics

2. If I was a sculptor, but then again no
   or a man who makes potions in a travelin' show…
   I know it's not much, but it's the best I can do.
   My gift is my song and this one's for you.

3. I sat on the roof and kicked off the moss.
   Well, a few of the verses well, they've got me quite cross.
   But the sun's been quite kind while I wrote this song.
   It's for people like you that keep it turned on.

4. So excuse me forgetting, but these things I do.
   You see I've forgotten if they're green, ha, or they're blue.
   Anyway, the thing is, what I really mean,
   Yours are the sweetest eyes I've ever seen.

Oh, Pretty Woman

Words and Music by Roy Orbison and Bill Dees

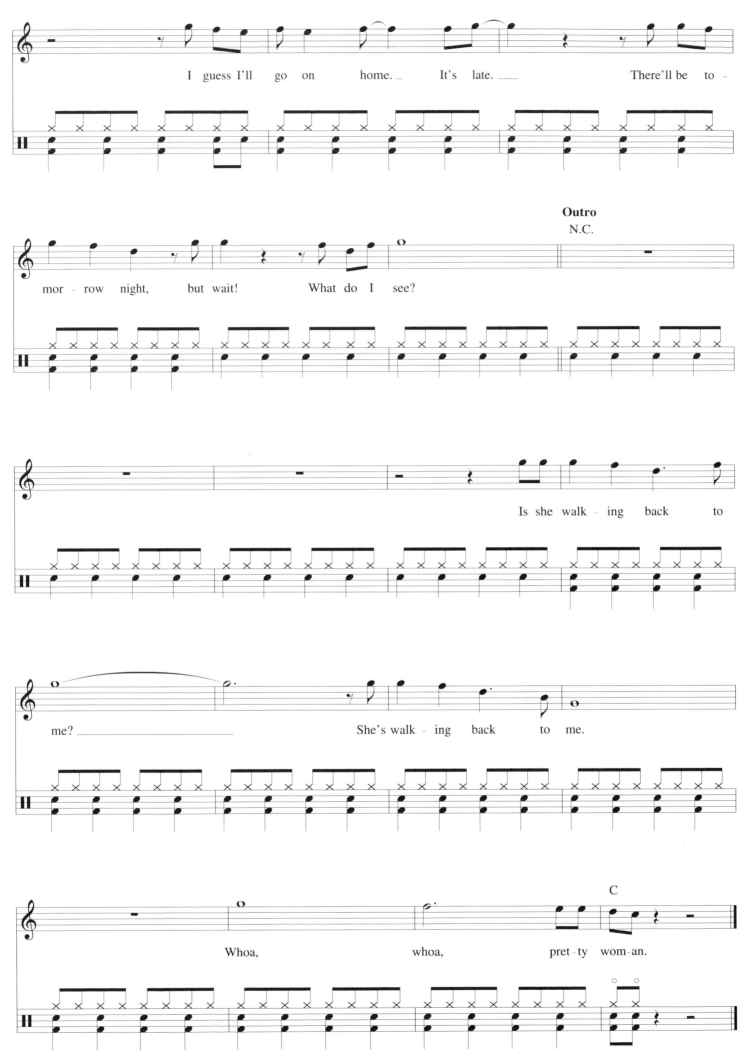

I guess I'll go on home. It's late. There'll be to-

Outro
N.C.

mor - row night, but wait! What do I see?

Is she walk - ing back to

me? She's walk - ing back to me.

C

Whoa, whoa, pret - ty wom-an.

Brown Eyed Girl

Words and Music by Van Morrison

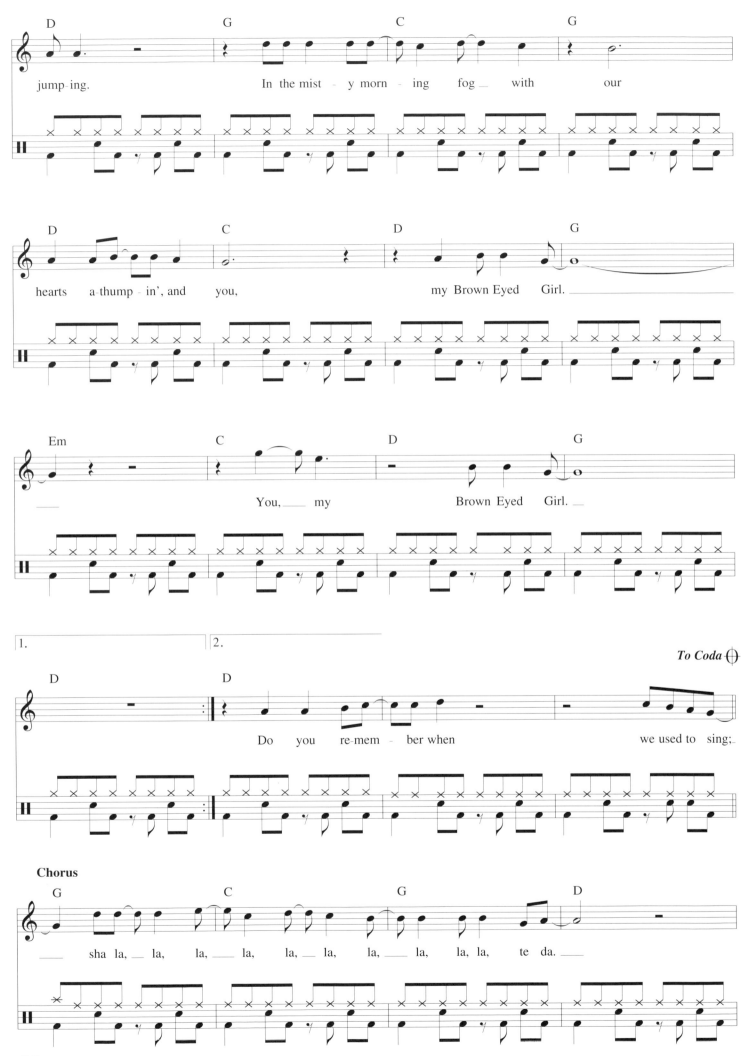

Additional Lyrics

2. Whatever happened to Tuesday and so slow
   Going down the old mine with a transistor radio
   Standing in the sunlight laughing
   Hiding behind a rainbow's wall
   Slipping and a–sliding
   All along the waterfall
   With you, my Brown Eyed Girl.
   You, my Brown Eyed Girl.
   Do you remember when we used to sing:
   Chorus

3. So hard to find my way, now that I'm all on my own
   I saw you just the other day, my, how you have grown
   Cast my memory back there, Lord
   Sometime I'm overcome thinking 'bout
   Making love in the green grass
   Behind the stadium
   With you, my Brown Eyed Girl
   With you, my Brown Eyed Girl.
   Do you remember when we used to sing:
   Chorus

Great Balls of Fire

Words and Music by Otis Blackwell and Jack Hammer

feels... good... Hold me ba - by! Well, ___

___ I wan-na love ya like a lov - er should. _ You're fine... _ so kind... _ I

Verse

got to tell this world that you're mine, mine, mine, mine. I chew my nails and I twid-dle my thumbs.

I'm real ner-vous but it sure is fun. _ Come on, ba - by, you drive me cra - zy,

good-ness, gra - cious, great _ balls of fire! _ balls of fire!

HAL·LEONARD®
DRUM PLAY-ALONG

AUDIO ACCESS INCLUDED

The Drum Play-Along™ Series will help you play your favorite songs quickly and easily! Just follow the drum notation, listen to the audio to hear how the drums should sound, and then play-along using the separate backing tracks. The lyrics are also included for reference. The audio files are enhanced so you can adjust the recording to any tempo without changing pitch!

1. Pop/Rock
00699742......................................$14.99

2. Classic Rock
00699741......................................$16.99

3. Hard Rock
00699743......................................$17.99

4. Modern Rock
00699744......................................$19.99

5. Funk
00699745......................................$16.99

7. Punk Rock
00699747......................................$14.99

8. '80s Rock
00699832......................................$16.99

9. Cover Band Hits
00211599......................................$16.99

10. blink-182
00699834......................................$19.99

11. Jimi Hendrix Experience: Smash Hits
00699835......................................$19.99

12. The Police
00700268......................................$16.99

13. Steely Dan
00700202......................................$17.99

15. The Beatles
00256656......................................$17.99

16. Blues
00700272......................................$17.99

17. Nirvana
00700273......................................$16.99

18. Motown
00700274......................................$16.99

19. Rock Band: Modern Rock Edition
00700707......................................$17.99

21. Weezer
00700959......................................$14.99

22. Black Sabbath
00701190......................................$17.99

23. The Who
00701191......................................$22.99

24. Pink Floyd – Dark Side of the Moon
00701612......................................$19.99

25. Bob Marley
00701703......................................$19.99

26. Aerosmith
00701887......................................$19.99

27. Modern Worship
00701921......................................$19.99

29. Queen
00702389......................................$17.99

30. Dream Theater
00111942......................................$24.99

31. Red Hot Chili Peppers
00702992......................................$19.99

32. Songs for Beginners
00704204......................................$15.99

33. James Brown
00117422......................................$17.99

34. U2
00124470......................................$19.99

35. Buddy Rich
00124640......................................$19.99

36. Wipe Out & 7 Other Fun Songs
00125341......................................$19.99

37. Slayer
00139861......................................$17.99

38. Eagles
00143920......................................$17.99

39. Kiss
00143937......................................$16.99

40. Stevie Ray Vaughan
00146155......................................$16.99

41. Rock Songs for Kids
00148113......................................$15.99

42. Easy Rock Songs
00148143......................................$15.99

45. Bon Jovi
00200891......................................$17.99

46. Mötley Crüe
00200892......................................$16.99

47. Metallica: 1983-1988
00234340......................................$19.99

48. Metallica: 1991-2016
00234341......................................$19.99

49. Top Rock Hits
00256655......................................$16.99

51. Deep Purple
00278400......................................$16.99

52. More Songs for Beginners
00278403......................................$14.99

53. Pop Songs for Kids
00298650......................................$15.99

HAL·LEONARD®

Visit Hal Leonard Online at
www.halleonard.com

Prices, contents and availability subject to change without notice and may vary outside the US.

HAL•LEONARD® DRUM PLAY-ALONG

AUDIO ACCESS INCLUDED

The Drum Play-Along™ Series will help you play your favorite songs quickly and easily! Just follow the drum notation, listen to the audio to hear how the drums should sound, and then play-along using the separate backing tracks. The lyrics are also included for reference. The audio files are enhanced so you can adjust the recording to any tempo without changing pitch!

1. Pop/Rock
00699742.............................$14.99

2. Classic Rock
00699741.............................$15.99

3. Hard Rock
00699743.............................$15.99

4. Modern Rock
00699744.............................$15.99

5. Funk
00699745.............................$15.99

6. '90s Rock
00699746.............................$17.99

7. Punk Rock
00699747.............................$14.99

8. '80s Rock
00699832.............................$15.99

9. Cover Band Hits
00211599.............................$16.99

10. blink-182
00699834.............................$16.99

11. Jimi Hendrix Experience: Smash Hits
00699835.............................$17.99

12. The Police
00700268.............................$16.99

13. Steely Dan
00700202.............................$16.99

15. The Beatles
00256656.............................$16.99

16. Blues
00700272.............................$16.99

17. Nirvana
00700273.............................$15.99

18. Motown
00700274.............................$15.99

19. Rock Band: Modern Rock Edition
00700707.............................$17.99

20. Rock Band: Classic Rock Edition
00700708.............................$14.95

21. Weezer
00700959.............................$14.99

22. Black Sabbath
00701190.............................$16.99

23. The Who
00701191.............................$16.99

24. Pink Floyd – Dark Side of the Moon
00701612.............................$16.99

25. Bob Marley
00701703.............................$17.99

26. Aerosmith
00701887.............................$15.99

27. Modern Worship
00701921.............................$16.99

28. Avenged Sevenfold
00702388.............................$17.99

29. Queen
00702389.............................$16.99

30. Dream Theater
00111942.............................$24.99

31. Red Hot Chili Peppers
00702992.............................$19.99

32. Songs for Beginners
00704204.............................$14.99

33. James Brown
00117422.............................$16.99

34. U2
00124470.............................$16.99

35. Buddy Rich
00124640.............................$19.99

36. Wipe Out & 7 Other Fun Songs
00125341.............................$16.99

37. Slayer
00139861.............................$17.99

38. Eagles
00143920.............................$16.99

39. Kiss
00143937.............................$16.99

40. Stevie Ray Vaughan
00146155.............................$16.99

41. Rock Songs for Kids
00148113.............................$14.99

42. Easy Rock Songs
00148143.............................$14.99

45. Bon Jovi
00200891.............................$16.99

46. Mötley Crüe
00200892.............................$16.99

47. Metallica: 1983-1988
00234340.............................$19.99

48. Metallica: 1991-2016
00234341.............................$19.99

49. Top Rock Hits
00256655.............................$16.99

51. Deep Purple
00278400.............................$16.99

52. More Songs for Beginners
00278403.............................$14.99

53. Pop Songs for Kids
00298650.............................$15.99

HAL•LEONARD®

Visit Hal Leonard Online at
www.halleonard.com